Music Therapy

Another path to learning and communication for children on the autism spectrum.

Betsey King, MMT, MT-BC

Music Therapy

All marketing and publishing rights guaranteed to and reserved by

721 W. Abram Street
Arlington, Texas 76013
800-489-0727
817-277-0727
817-277-2270 (fax)
E-mail: info@FHautism.com
www.FHautism.com

ISBN 1-885477-53-8

Table of Contents

Introduction v

About the Author vii

Acknowledgements ix

How to Use This Book xi

Part I: What is Music Therapy? 1

    Important Notes 2

    Music Therapy Is 3

    Music Therapy is Prescribed 4

    A Qualified Music Therapist 6

    The Relationship that Develops 7

    The Music in Music Therapy 8

    To Assist or Motivate 9

    Achieving Non-Musical Goals 10

    A Music Therapist Works as Part of a Team 12

    Summary 13

Part II: Nine Therapeutic Characteristics of Music 15

    1. Music Captivates and Maintains Attention 16

    2. Music Structures Time 39

    3. Music is Success-Oriented 48

    4. Music Provides a Safe Place to Practice Social Skills 57

    5. Music Makes Repetition and Memorization Enjoyable 65

    6. Music Lets Children Control Their Environment 75

    7. Music Can Create or Emphasize a Routine 83

    8. Music Can Reflect and Adapt to Each Individual 89

    9. Music is Movable 93

Part III: Music Therapy Services 101

References 111

Introduction

Music is a unique path to communication and learning for children with autism. Its effectiveness as a therapeutic and learning tool comes from its ability to provide two distinct frameworks for therapy and teaching. Music can create a consistent, stable, and predictable environment. Melody, harmony, and rhythm from a favorite song can provide familiar cues and bring comfort in an unfamiliar or stressful setting. Yet music can also be infinitely flexible: changing with the child from moment to moment, reflecting his or her behavior and emotions.

Music therapy is the prescribed use of music to address non-musical goals in such areas as cognition, communication, and socialization. Music therapists are degree professionals who structure specific therapeutic plans in a variety of educational and health care settings, creating unique interventions for each individual. However, many of the principles of music therapy can be put to use by other therapists, teachers, and parents—*even by people who do not consider themselves musical.*

This book outlines some of the principles of music therapy and provides sample music therapy strategies for use with children on the autism spectrum are provided. Research references and sources for materials. In each chapter, there are suggestions for how you can put this information to use. This book is based on my experiences as a music therapist and on the current research in music therapy. It is not comprehensive, but it will provide examples and starting points. The next steps in the journey will be up to you.

About the Author

Betsey King, MMT, MT-BC is a board-certified music therapist who began her practice in 1984. She has an undergraduate degree in violin performance from the University of Cincinnati College Conservatory of Music and a masters degree in music therapy from Southern Methodist University in Dallas, Texas. She spent eight years as the music therapist at Baylor University Medical Center in Dallas, and eight years working with children with special needs in special education and private practice. In 2000, she moved into university teaching and has trained music therapy students at Southern Methodist University and the University of Kansas. In 2006, she joined the faculty of Nazareth College in Rochester, New York. Betsey speaks and leads workshops throughout the United States, and is the co-owner and co-author for Prelude Music Therapy Products.

Acknowledgements

I could not have finished this book without the help of colleagues, friends, and family. In particular, I'd like to thank my business partner and friend, Kathleen Coleman for her tireless support and contributions; and Wayne Gilpin, for giving me so many opportunities to share these ideas.

Every child with whom I've worked has taught me something important about the role of music in learning and growing. I hope I can communicate those experiences effectively.

This book is dedicated to Alexander Jackson King.

How to Use This Book

Throughout this book you will find two features that will help you incorporate music therapy ideas into your home, classroom or therapy setting.

PLAY ALONG boxes suggest specific things that you can do to apply the information in each chapter.

SONGS AND VISUAL AID PATTERNS from prelude music therapy will help you see how music therapy strategies can be applied to simple goals and objectives.

In addition to these features, this book includes a resource list for equipment, related books and supplies and a list of the prelude music therapy material that include the sample songs and visual aids featured in this text. Also included is information on workshops and presentations you can schedule for further exploration of music therapy; and some helpful phone numbers and internet resources.

Part I: What is Music Therapy?

Definitions, Qualifications, & Applications

Important Notes

This section provides basic information about music therapy as a profession. An understanding of the principles of music therapy will help you understand many of the recommendations that appear in this book.

Music therapists work in a variety of settings: in medical and psychiatric facilities, nursing homes, long-term care centers and public and private schools. Many music therapists work in private practice, doing a combination of individual and group sessions and, perhaps, consultation. *For the purposes of this book, I will refer only to the work music therapists do with persons with developmental disabilities, specifically autism, and to the situations in which that work takes place.*

You do not have to be a music therapists to use music in teaching, therapy, or parenting. There are specific circumstances in which you will want to find a qualified music therapists. These are outlined later in the book. However, there are many steps you can take on your own; becoming your own musical investigator and applying some of the tenets of music therapy to benefit those with whom you work and live.

Music is a part of all of our lives—and most of the time, we have no need to think about its application or specific effects. However when we are concerned with improving our connection to children in the autism spectrum and helping them gain important skills, we do need to think about how we are using music in educational and therapeutic environments.

Music Therapy is:

 the prescribed use (by a qualified music therapist) of music, and the relationship that develops through shared musical experiences, to assist or motivate a person to achieve non-musical goals.

Music Therapy is Prescribed

Some music is just for fun. Many children love to sing silly songs while making funny faces and dancing around the room. (Some adults do, too!) Some music is introduced into the environment for an overall positive effect—like a fight song at a football game or the quiet music we play when it is time to rest. Store owners play familiar music, hoping to entice their customers to linger.

Music therapy, on the other hand, focuses on individuals and specific individual needs. A music therapist identifies particular, non-musical goals for a student, then chooses and creates music designed to address those goals. The MT-BC (board-certified music therapist) makes a time-specific plan for working on goals, documents the student's responses and progress, and makes changes as necessary. Music therapy is modified or discontinued when it is not having an impact on the specific goals and objectives for which it was introduced.

Music therapy begins with an assessment. Depending on the setting, the assessment can take many forms: It can be done through the administration of test items, and it can be accomplished through observation of the student's participation. The outcome is a documented plan for therapy, with goals and objectives specific to the music therapy sessions and a plan for regularly evaluating the therapy's effectiveness.

Sometimes a music therapist acts as a consultant to another therapist or teacher. In these cases, a formal assessment may not be completed, and the goals and objectives identified may be those already addressed by that therapist or educator. However, whenever music therapy strategies are introduced, the music therapist has the responsibility to document their use and regularly evaluate their impact.

PLAY ALONG:

If you would like more information on the process of music therapy assessments, especially those for public schools, please visit the Prelude Music Therapy website at www. preludemusictherapy.com *before* you request an assessment or related services.

A Qualified Music Therapist

Music therapists are trained at the undergraduate and graduate levels at colleges and university programs approved by the American Music Therapy Association (AMTA www.musictherapy.org). Students in these programs complete a rigorous program of coursework that includes music performance classes, a comprehensive overview of psychology, statistics, anatomy and physiology and a series of music therapy courses are accompanied by clinical training in health and education sites in the area.

Once a student has completed this coursework (4-5 years for an undergraduate or its equivalent), he or she must complete an internship that lasts several months. The internship is supervised by a qualified music therapist and takes place at a site specifically approved for such clinical training by the American Music Therapy Association

The final stage in music therapy qualifications is passing a national board Certification Board For Music Therapists (CBMT). The exam tests potential therapists in, among other things, the areas of music knowledge, clinical interventions, and professionals ethics.

A music therapist seeking a master's degree will complete specialized study in music therapy and publish a thesis or professional project. **All music therapists who have completed their educational and clinical training and passed the board certification exam will use the professional designation MT-BC.**

The Relationship That Develops

People who play in instrumental ensembles or sing in a choir or other group will tell you that there is a special energy that comes through musical communication. Making a connection without using words—through melody, rhythm and harmony—can be a thrill.

When one has difficulty with verbal communication, such a connection can be even more significant. Music can be a bridge: for an adult who is aphasic after a stroke, a teenager who has not had success in expressing himself, or a child on the autism spectrum. If such a bridge is created, the person who helped with its construction may be seen as someone safe, someone who can be trusted.

Music therapists may have an important role in teaching or treatment when trust has been established through shared musical experiences. Difficult tasks and issues can be presented through music, and the music therapist can assist other members of the team to use the music throughout the educational or therapeutic environment. When a child in the autism spectrum responds positively to music, it makes sense to let that child establish and explore relationships and learning through musical activities.

The Music in Music Therapy

Music affects each of us differently. Although researchers are making strides in identifying areas in which music or music training is influential, no replicated research has shown that a particular type or style of music affects all its listeners in the same way. Some recorded music is marketed with claims of "healing" or "accelerated learning," and for some people, music may have positive effects. There are no studies, however, that have identified particular music as being beneficial to all children in the autism spectrum.

A music therapist, therefore, uses a wide variety of music in therapy sessions and constantly observes a child's response to music. The music therapists primary use is live music, so that variations can be made even within a single song if that will provide the optimum opportunity for the child with autism to make progress on his or her goals.

For example, some children need more time than others to respond. A recording of a song may not provide ample time for a child to process information and act on it. The music therapist playing live music can pause for whatever amount of time is needed—and can adjust the pause time to help the child increase the need of response. Some children have low voices, others high ones. If the music therapist plays music live, he or she can adjust the key of the song to match the child's vocal range. Live music can also be adjusted if it becomes over stimulating.

To Assist or Motivate

The many ways in which our brain processes and produces music are far from being fully understood. Research, especially that which focuses on people who have had specific brain damage, has begun to identify parts of the brain associated with such skills as melody recognition and production, rhythm, and physical production of music on an instrument. It is far from being a left brain/right brain distinction: music processing is found throughout the brain.

Part of what this means is that music can both assist AND motivate a person to perform function tasks. When a person with aphasia brought on by a stroke or brain injury is able to produce words through singing that she cannot through speech, music might be said to be assisting her in this task. On the other hand, when that same person agrees to participate in an exercise group because her favorite music will be played, music can be seen as a motivating factor.

With what we are learning about the mind-body connection, even such a simple distinction is becoming blurred. The important thing to remember is that participation in music often goes beyond basic enjoyment. It can have a significant impact on our ability to function in daily life.

Achieving Non-Musical Goals

This is perhaps, the most important part of the definition of music therapy. Music therapy focuses on non-musical goals. This is what distinguishes it from music education, music lessons, and recreational music.

Learning about music, and learning to play an instrument, can have positive effects. Studies have shown that learning to play the piano has helped some children improve their scores on specific parts of the standard IQ test. Other studies have indicated that the discipline involved in learning an instrument carries over into other parts of the student's life. Certainly, the ability to play an instrument provides a child with unique opportunities for community involvement and peer interaction.

When a child with autism shows interest in playing an instrument and is able to participate in music lessons (perhaps with some modifications), he or she should be encouraged and supported in doing so. Singing and playing instruments can be a path towards increased inclusion and self-esteem.

Music Therapy, however, is a different approach. It does not take the place of music education and, in fact, it may co-exist with music lessons as a part of a child's life. Music therapy uses a person's interest in, and enjoyment of, music to help that person make changes in specific, non-musical areas of his of her life.

A music therapist may teach a student to play an instrument, but in that case, musical learning is not the primary purpose of therapy. In special education settings, goal areas likely to be addressed by a music therapist include attention span, fine motor skills, self- care skills, academic work, social skills and expressive and receptive communication.

IMPORTANT NOTE: If music therapy is found, through a valid assessment process, to be a necessary related service for a student, music therapy must be included on his or her IEP. The student may participate in music classes, but this does not address specific non-musical goals derived from his or her individual educational plan.

PLAY ALONG

1. For more information about adapted music lessons, including questions you can ask to see if they would be appropriate for your child or student, please see Part III: Music Therapy Services.

2. At the back of this book you will find some reference materials for future reading on the subject of music therapy and music therapy research. Most of these texts and journal articles can be found at a university or college that offers a degree in music therapy. For the locations of those schools, contact the American Music Therapy Association (301) 589-3300.

A Music Therapist Works as Part of a Team

One important point has not been mentioned in the definition of music therapy. A music therapist works as part of a team. In an educational setting, this means that the music therapist is an active member of the IEP committee. In private practice, this means that the music therapist actively seeks information from a student's family and from the professionals who are involved in his or her therapy and/or education.

Throughout this book, I will give examples of ways in which music has been an effective tool. Sometimes, the effects of music therapy are immediate; most often, they come over time. In almost every case, however, many people—most importantly the students themselves – contribute to a result. The occupational therapist designs a splint that supports an arm or hand. The physical therapist's work makes it possible for the student to sit upright during therapy. Parents and classroom teachers provide important information about the student's learning, environmental, and musical preferences.

Music therapists frequently work hand-in-hand with speech language therapists. Music, language, and movement are intertwined in a child's development. When development is altered in some way, music may cure speech and provide nonverbal ways of communicating. The ultimate goal, however, is for the child to be able to communicate without the musical support, so coordination with a communication specialist is critical.

Summary

- Music therapy is prescribed for a particular purpose.

- Music therapists are degreed, certified professionals.

- Music therapists use live, specially chosen music.

- Music therapy is for non-musical goals.

- Music therapists work as part of a team.

Part II:

Nine Therapeutic Characteristics of Music

The following chapters will introduce you to nine ways in which you can use music to facilitate learning and communication.

Each chapter contains examples from my clinical experiences and sample strategies for you to use in teaching, therapy and parenting.

Music Captivates and Maintains Attention

How many children in the autism spectrum do you know for whom "improving attention span" or "increasing on-task behavior" is a goal? Finding an environment in which a child with autism is tuned in without being over-stimulated is a challenge. Music-structured activities can be the answer.

The rhythm of music provides a focal point for attention: current research indicates that we may sense rhythm at a cellular level. Providing a steady beat may help a child organize his or her environment. Changing rhythm to match a child's activity level may help the child stay with a task longer. The rhythmic, melodic and harmonic consistency of familiar songs can create situations in which simple silence can be a cue for attention.

When Music is Used Effectively

- It **orients** students toward a teacher, therapist or parent.

- It **alerts** students that important information is coming.

- It **helps** students refocus if their attention wanders.

A classroom can be chaotic for a child on the autism spectrum. Posters on the walls and interesting spaces in between them, the sounds from a group of children in the hall outside, and the sounds of coughing from the child siting at the next desk can all be interesting and/or distracting.

The home environment can be equally challenging with the dog barking in the back yard, the sound of a toilet flushing upstairs, the way the sunlight is filtering through the blinds, or the face of an unfamiliar visitor.

The first step toward learning and communication, therefore, is helping a child focus on the information that is important. Several "acoustic" therapies have been created to help children in the autism spectrum learn to filter, tolerate, and/or prioritize the sound frequencies around them. Although many of these techniques have children listen to recorded music, they are a separate category from music therapy.

Music is a potent cue, especially when it is chosen to be distinct from the sounds already in the environment. I recently completed an assessment in a life-skills class at local high school. The students, all of whom had severe disabilities, were called to the morning orientation sessions with a tape recording of a bugle call. As the tape started, I noticed that several students looked towards the music, others got up and began moving toward the area for the activity. Almost every student demonstrated that he or she recognized that another part of their day was about to begin. The pitch and quality of the bugle sound, while not piercing, was distinct from the rather considerable ambient noise of the classroom, it was age-appropriate for the class (as opposed to a children's song), and it was brief—it did not last long enough to become just another sound in the overall environment.

The Contact Song

One of the first things a music therapist usually looks for in working with a new student or students is a CONTACT SONG. The contact song might be a pre-planned song. It might be a song composed on the spot, reflecting something the student is doing, or it might be a song that the therapist has been told is one of the student's favorites.

"Contact Song" (a term used by Edith Boxill in her book *Music Therapy for the Devolpmentally Disabled*) is a term for the music that accompanies the first connection with a student: the moment when reciprocal communication first takes place. That communication might be eye contact, the acceptance of a touch, singing, smiling: any signal the child chooses that indicates his or her active participation.

Several years ago, I was hired to provide music therapy-related services for a boy in the local school system. I was taking over the work from another therapist who had to give up the contract.

The young man, then age 8, was autistic, and had significant difficulties working on any task for more than a few seconds. The school personnel, at the time, had little training in working with someone with his needs and often placed him alone in a classroom with a teacher and an aide.

In talking with me about this student, the previous music therapist shared their contact song—"I Have a dinosaur." This was a simple color identification song that she sang while showing various colored shapes to the student and their moment of contact came when she showed him an orange jack-o-lantern shape and sang, "I Have a Pumpkin—its color is orange.

The student had thereafter greeted her each day with the words, "Candle! Candle!" She soon realized that this was his way of asking for the pumpkin song (as a candle is found inside a jack-o-lantern). On days when the young man was particularly anxious or over-stimulated, she had found that this song allowed him to focus and calm himself.

So, as we went over the transfer information for him, the therapist gave me the pumpkin shape and sang me the song.

On my first day in the young man's classroom, he was quite upset. He was already having a difficult day and the presence of a stranger did not help. For the first few minutes after I arrived, he ran around the room, taking things off shelves and throwing them to the floor. I attempted to engage him with a greeting song, then with some rhythm instruments.

Finally, I sat down at a small table and pulled the pumpkin shape out of my bag. Within 3 seconds of my beginning to sing "I Have A Pumpkin," the student was seated across from me, holding the pumpkin shape, making frequent eye contact, and singing along.

"I Have a Dinosaur"
appears at the end of this chapter.

In order to make music work for you in gaining and maintaining a child's attention, you will want to remember these three words:

 # Rhythm    # Discretion    # Silence

Rhythm. If I sang an otherwise familiar song but held each note for an inconsistent, unpredictable amount of time, not only would the song become almost unrecognizable—you might lose the interest or ability to focus on my singing.

Ooooooohhh, saycanyouseeeeeeeeee, by ......the-dawn's eeeearly....lightwhatsoproudly weeeeeeee......hailedatthe twiiiiiiiiiiiii.......light's lastgleeeeeeeeeeeeming.

Rhythm, the arrangement of notes around a steady beat, provides an important focal point.

I saw a demonstration of this when I did an assessment for a student who was not meeting the goal of reading aloud. I read him a book that had short phrases that could be presented rhythmically.

As I read, I snapped my fingers to create a beat. When I was finished, I gave him the book and asked him to read aloud. I tried a variety of verbal and gestural prompts but, although he was looking at the book and turning the pages, he was not speaking.

I turned the book back to the first page and, without saying anything, began to snap my fingers. Immediately, he began reading out loud.

PLAY ALONG

Picture books that illustrate songs, and book that can be read rhythmically, are wonderful tools for encouraging students to work on such goals as word recognition, reading, tracking, and using speech. Some books that you might enjoy using are:

Charlie Parker Played Be-Bop
by Chris Raschka (Orchard Books, 1992, ISBN 0-531059-99-5)

What A Wonderful World
by George Davis Weiss, Bob Thiele; illustrated by Ashley Bryan
(Atheneum, 1995, ISBN 0-689800-87-8)

Take Me Out To The Ball Game
by Jack Norworth; illustrated by Alex Gillman
(Four Winds, 1993, ISBN 0-027359-91-3)

Chika-Chika Boom-Boom
by Bill Martin, Jr, John Achambault; illustrated by Lois Ehlert
(Simon & Schuster, 1989, ISBN 0-671679-49-X)

Worksong
by Gary Paulsen, illustrated by Ruth Wright Paulsen
(Harcourt Brace & Company, 1997, ISBN 0-152009-80-9)

Discretion. Do you listen to your refrigerator? Most readers will answer "no" this question, yet their refrigerators are making noise all day long. Because the noise is so familiar and constant, however, most of us have blocked it out of our conscious attention.

If you work in an office where music is piped in over a speaker system, do you attentively listen to each song? "Background music" is meant not be a kind of aural wallpaper. You don't notice the individual songs and usually can't recall what was played later. However, if you work in an office without music, and each day a person came and played live, one or two songs, you would probably pay much closer attention to music, remembering the words, and perhaps humming fragments of the melodies later in the day.

If you want a child with autism to be able to use music for learning and communication, make sure that music doesn't become part of the background and lose its potency as a stimulus and focal point. Pick those tasks with which the student is having the most difficulty and try using music for those specific times of day.

Silence is part of the equation, too - music and silence provide a powerful nonverbal cue. If you've ever been listening to the radio and had the station go off the air suddenly, you've experienced one aspect of this phenomenon. The sudden silence can be more of a stimulus than the music was. For another example of the power of silence, try singing "Happy Birthday" without the last note.

Happy Birthday to you,
Happy Birthday to you,
Happy Birthday dear Suzy,
Happy Birthday to - -

You need to finish it, don't you? There is something intrinsically uncomfortable about stopping before the song is completed. in this case, silence is a poor substitute for the preferred stimulus and it creates a motivation for us to finish the song.

So how does this work in the classroom? Here is an example of the way in which I use silence as a cue:

I have a song that I have adapted to address the goal of matching initial consonant sounds with the words they begin. It's called "The Letter Bears" and you can find it at the end of this chapter.

When I'm working with a group of children, there will inevitably be ebbs and flows in their attention. Once they are familiar with a song like "The Letter Bears," however, I can use sudden pauses to startle them into refocusing. Instead of:

Bobby, take a heart
A heart that has a "P"
And put it on the Letter Bear
The bear whose name starts with "P."

What you might hear is:

Bobby take heart
A heart that
[silence]
has a "P"
And put it in the Letter Bear
The [silence]
The Bear whose name starts with "P"

Those silences are silent. No verbal cue, no physical prompt. With 9 out of 10 Bobbys I am going to get a reaction. At first, he'll simply refocus on me to find out where the music went! The instant that he returns his attention to me, however, I start up right where I left off. No comment, just music. After a certain number of repetitions, he will get the idea that, if he wants the song to continue, he must maintain his attention.

This usually works when the child is familiar with the song. It makes sense—you will not necessarily know that a song has been interrupted unless you know what it is supposed to sound like when complete.

Silence in the midst of music can also create a cue for communication or social behavior. I have a greeting song that I use at the start of most school sessions. (It is printed at the end of this chapter.)

After the students learn the song, I pause after I sing "Hello, [Name], Hello," In this pause, depending on the student, I put out my hand for a handshake or say "hi" and wait for a verbal response. We don't go on until the students participate in whatever way they are able, and the silence reminds them of this. The important aspect of this strategy is that the student initiates the behavior or behavior change, rather than the teacher or therapist.

When students are part of a music-making group, like a bell choir (see page 50), silence from one person who has missed his or her note may cause the students to cue each other, helping them learn responsibility and consideration, and to recognize and value a group identity.

When I present this information in front of a live audience, this is the point at which many people start to look anxious. If I ask them what is bothering them, the answer is:

"I can't sing!"

Some of you reading this may be making the same statement but never fear: There are several things you can do to feel more comfortable about singing. The most important thing to remember, though, is that when you sing, your students (or child) will associate you—and not some faceless voice from recording—with the positive musical experience. It is worth it, therefore, to improve your ability to sing. Here are three ways to do it:

Sing in the range of your speaking voice.

Many people feel uncomfortable singing because they are straining for the notes. It doesn't help that quite a lot of music is written so that you have to sing outside your comfort zone. You will have more success singing if you sing songs with the same pitches with which you speak. Try this: say "la, la, la." Now, simple extend each syllable so that you are holding it for a second or two: "laaaa, laaaa, laaaa." This is what it should feel like when you are singing a song. If the songs you are using for your children are not in comfortable keys, ask a musical friend (the music teacher at school, or a musician from your house of worship) to record them in a range that is better for you.

Practice supporting your voice and finding/holding notes.

The easiest way to do is to sing in the car. You're alone (at least some of the time), you have radio/tape-player/CD player to provide music, and you will be using your time effectively! As you sing, think about how you are breathing. If your breathing is shallow, and your voice seems to come from a place no lower than your neck, then you are likely to be singing with a lot of air. It will be more difficult to control the notes you hit. Hold them once you hit them, and your voice will get tired quickly. On the other hand, if you breathe deeply (when you do this, your diaphragm gets involved and you'll see your tummy push out), you will give your voice more support. Remember, if you are singing along with one of the female pop or country stars, you may want to sing an octave lower than she does—keeping your singing in the range of your speaking voice.

Sing more slowly and more loudly.

If you are not comfortable with your voice, this may seem like bad advice. What you will find, though, is that a song sung tentatively and in a rushed manner sounds worse than a song sung with confidence. Think of Rex Harrison in *My Fair Lady*. His ability to sing led him to talk his way through many of the songs. He did it, however, with confidence and style and when he did sing melody, he did not hesitate or hold back. When you use therapy in music or teaching, you will discover that your students respond more consistently and enthusiastically to you when you are willing to sing with similar confidence.

Summary

- Music orients students, alerts them to important information, and can cue them to refocus attention.

- A Contact Song can help a child feel safe and oriented.

- Rhythm provides an important stimulus and helps children focus their attention on a task.

- Use discretion when using music for learning and therapy; choose specific tasks to which you will add music.

- Silence in the midst of familiar music can provide a powerful cue.

- Children will pay more attention to you if you sing with confidence, no matter what your skill level is.

I Have A Dinosaur

Music: Folk Melody
Words: K. Coleman, MMT, MT-BC

I have a di-no-saur whose co - lor is

(co - lor). I have a di-no-saur whose co-lor is

(co - lor). I have a di-no-saur whose co - lor is

(co - lor). I have a di-no -saur who walks like

this. Pat legs, make walking sound at end of song.

Hello Everybody

B. Brunk, MMT, MT-BC

Hel - lo, (na - me), hel - lo! I am glad that you are here to - day. Hel - lo, (na - me), he - lo! I am glad that you're here to - day.

(Na - me), (na - me) (clap your hands). (Clap your hands) oh (clap your hands). (Na - me), (na - me) (clap your hands). I am glad you are here to - day.

The Letter Bears

The next pages provide music and a pattern for a tagboard book taken from Prelude Music Therapy Visual Aids Kit, Volume 2. Use the illustration on the next page for the cover of the book, the named bears as the pages, and the music as the back of the book. Copy the letter hearts onto card stock. Enlarge as necessary. Color, if desired, with markers or colored pencils. Laminate everything and use Velcro™ to attach the hearts to the appropriate bears.

The Letter Bears

Les

Fred

Yaz

Ann

Jan

Ed

Ken

Tom

Bill

Greg

Will

Cal

Mo

Pat

Sue

Dan

Von

Ike

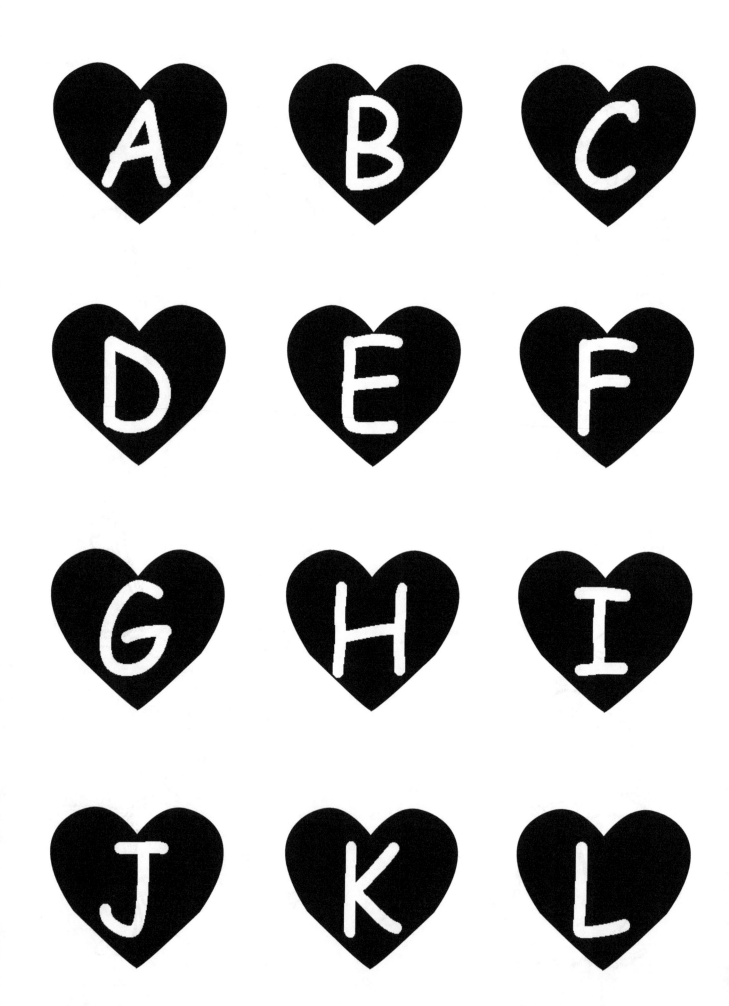

The Letter Bears

B. Brunk, RMT-BC

Music Structures Time

Have you ever taken an aerobics class? Can you imagine doing it without music? Aerobics instructors use music for a variety of reasons: The rhythm of the music helps participants coordinate their movements, and the upbeat and familiar nature of the music creates a pleasant atmosphere.

An interesting thing happens, however, when you are straining to complete a particular part of the routine. You find yourself listening to the music and getting a clear idea of how much longer you have to go ("Okay, just one more verse, and then the last chorus, and then I'll be done.")

Children do the same thing when their learning and communication tasks are structured with music. For children who have difficulty maintaining focus or who are easily frustrated, the knowledge of exactly how long they will need to work is invaluable. For children, music is a way they can understand the passage of time.

Consider a repetitive task. For many children with developmental disabilities, one of the effective methods of teaching is through repetition. Yet a difficult task, done over and over again, can cause frustration, even when the teacher is careful to provide positive feedback and encouragement.

Within a song, however, you can present a piece of information several times without it becoming boring and, if you have let your students help you find apiece of music that you will enjoy, you will see that they adjust their concentration and participation to match the length of the song.

An example of such a song is "I Sign More" (printed at the end of this chapter). It provides the student with nine opportunities to practice a particular sign, and it would work equally well if the goal was a single spoken word. The repetitions of the task flow as part of the natural "waltz" rhythm of the piece.

Some of the students who play rhythm instruments in my sessions are trying to get accustomed to holding an object for longer and longer periods of time. That is why each rhythm instrument has a song that I always play after handing the instrument to the student. The song, initially, is brief (only 4 short lines) and simple. In just a few sessions, a student like this will hold and/or play the instrument for exactly the amount of time it takes me to finish the song. As I reach the last note and sing "and stop!"—he or she will be handing me the instrument in perfect coordination with the last chord.

I have seen students for whom a goal was the act of holding their heads upright. One would not consider these students "musicians," and yet they understand the structure of the songs well enough to maintain their head control for exactly the length of the song. No more, no less.

Chords/Harmony

Chords (Harmony)- are a big part of the way in which we understand the structure of a song. In Western music, most popular songs are written around three different chords. These chords (groups of three or more notes played together), are built upon three of the notes in a scale (do-re-mi-fa-sol-la-ti-do).

The three chords will be designated by the letter name of their lowest note (A-G) or by a roman numeral that indicates the position of that note in the scale. The three chords that form the basis for most songs are I, IV, and V—chords that start on the first, fourth and fifth notes of the scale.

If the song is written around the scale that goes from C to C:

C-D-E-F-G-A-B-C

the three chords in the song are almost always going to be the ones that start on the notes C, F, and G (I, IV, V). Most importantly, the first and last chords will always be the "I" chord. If you also can remember that the second to last chord will almost always be the V chord (the one based on G, the fifth note), then you know most of what you need to know about harmony.

```
C                 F   C
Twinkle, twinkle little star
```

```
F    C    G       C
How I wonder what you are
```

If you stop the song on the second to last note/chord, you will, as we discussed earlier, feel very uncomfortable. It's that sense of anticipation that children are using to know when a song is over.

Autoharp/Omnichord

Harmony isn't always necessary, but it can play significant part in the effectiveness of a therapeutic song. If you don't play the guitar or piano, you may be wondering how you can produce harmony to accompany your singing. The autoharp and its electronic counterpart, the omnichord are solutions to this problem. Both instruments have buttons labeled with the letter names of chords. You simply press the button and the chord is created. To make it sound, you strum the strings of the autoharp, or the metal strip on one side of the omnichord.

Omnichord

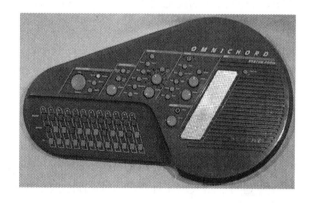

Autoharp

Music therapist also use the concept of music structuring time when they program a music therapy sessions, I start every session with a greeting song appropriate to the ages of the students (My "Hello" song is printed at the end of the previous chapter). This is often followed by orientation songs, or songs that single out each member of a group. After that, we move onto the music therapy strategies that I have chosen to address the students' goals. Before the end of the sessions, I usually will sing either a silly song (just for fun!) or a quiet song that will encourage the students to make a peaceful transition into their next activity. Finally, I conclude with a "goodbye song." As the students become familiar with this sequence, it provides them with the security of knowing what is coming, and how long it will take. Many of my students develop an internal clock that allows them to work at their highest level for a consistent period of time.

Here are two sample "session plans."

• **Opening Song**
• **Name Song**
• **How Are You?**
• **[Goal-oriented strategy]**
• **[Goal-oriented strategy with rhythm instruments]**
• **[Goal-oriented strategy]**
• **Quiet song**
• **Goodbye**

• **Opening Song**
• **Favorites**
• **Calendar Songs**
• **[Goal-oriented strategy]**
• **[Goal-oriented strategy with instruments]**
• **[Goal-oriented strategy]**
• **Silly song**
• **Goodbye**

Summary

- Music structures time in a way that a child can understand.

- Children will pace themselves and control frustration when they have to work.

- Harmony is an important part of the way in which children understand the structure of a song. Omnichords and autoharps provide a way for people who don't have musical training to accompany themselves as they sing.

- Using a regular sequence of music within a "session" can help students work effectively for longer periods of time.

I Sign "More"

K. Coleman, MMT-BC

Suggestions:

This song is useful for providing repetitive practice on basic communicative signs in the student's vocabulary. Additional verse might include:

When I'm hungry and ready for lunch (or dinner or breakfast) I sign "eat" , etc.
When I'm hungry and I want a snack, I sign "eat" , etc.

When there is a problem and I need some help, I sign "help", etc.
When I don't understand and I just don't know how, I sign "help", etc.

When my work is don't and I want to stop, I sign "finished" , etc.
When I've done the task enough is enough, I sign "finished" , etc.

Days of the Week

Today is...

Betsey King Brunk, MMT-BC

Music is
Success-Oriented

If you can hear music—or even sense its beat and vibrations—you can participate in musical experiences. If you can produce a single note, you can have a pivotal role in the production of music. Music therapists use these facts to involve children with disabilities in music when an observer might assume that these children do not have the skills required for musical expression.

When a student has difficulty in many areas of her life finds that she is successful in music, music becomes a highly motivating and preferred activity for her. She then may be willing to spend time working on non-musical tasks if they are structured or accompanied by music.

Here's an example of how one small physical movement can be critical to the successful completion of a song.

When teaching my students about the various rooms in a house, I often use a song called "My Little Parrot." The song is printed at the end of this chapter.

As I write this book, I have a student who has severe cognitive and physical disabilities. She has one fairly consistent voluntary motor skill: She can move her right hand in an up-and-down motion. Her head control is inconsistent, she is not ambulatory, and she does not demonstrate the use of any communication system. One would not expect her to be an important member of a musical group, or to participate effectively in a group with students who have significantly higher-level goals.

When we sing the "Parrot" song, however, I place a single-click switch under her right hand. The switch allows me to record a short phrase, and I record myself singing the last two words of the song; "Big Mouth!" Then I sing the song to/with the group. When we reach the end, I stop abruptly after " gee that little parrot has a—" Unless she presses on the switch, we cannot finish the song. There is usually a short pause, and then we hear the final two words. The other students clap, and she gets a big smile on her face.

Saying or singing the final word in a phrase; playing a rhythm instrument; keeping eye contact with a picture song book—these are all ways in which students can participate in music.

PLAY ALONG

Look at the music you are using in the classroom or home. Think about how you can help your child or students become more actively involved in singing or playing.

Choir Chimes/Resonator Bells

Choir chimes and resonator bells are another way that the act of playing a single note can be part of a large musical experience. Choir chimes are held in one hand and jerked downward: The mallet attached to the metal tube strikes the tube and creates a sound not unlike a hand bell. Resonator bells come in sets and look like xylophones—but each bell is separate.

There are many ways to have students perform music with these instruments. If the students can match letters, you can provide cards or a chart that show each note in the order it needs to be played. "This Land Is Your Land," for example, would be notated

G-A-B-C   C   C-G-A-B   B

If the students can match colors, you can place colored dots on the bells and provide cards or charts with colors instead of letters. If the students cannot use a visual cue, you can stand behind them and tap them on the shoulder when it is time for them to play.

Handchime

Resonator
Bells

Song Writing

Another way that children can participate significantly in making music is through song writing. Song writing can be as simple as making a choice between two words—   or as complicated as writing lyrics and making choices about melody, harmony, rhythm and instrumentation.

A song like "Ravioli" (printed at the end of this chapter) is an example of simple song writing. Students can choose items of clothing by naming them, or by selecting a picture. Without their choice, the song is incomplete. The "Ohhhh" at the end of each verse, especially when it is accompanied by a silly face and waving arms, is something the students want to hear; so they make their choices quickly.

You can use existing songs as the basis for song writing simply by adding new words on top of the familiar melody. "How Are You," from the next chapter, is an example of this. You can "rap" a song and this will relieve you of the need to come up with a melody. Or, you can have more advanced students write lyrics to a "blues" progression:

E   E
The first line of words goes here - the second line goes here

E   E
The third line goes here - and some more words go here;

B7   A   E
We've got the blues   We've got the_____blues!"

51

Summary

- Listening—paying attention to music—is active participation.

- The ability to make one simple movement or one single sound is enough to make you an important part of a musical group.

- Choir chimes, resonator bells and song writing are ways to encourage active participation in music.

Goodbye

B. Brunk, RMT-BC

My Little Parrot

Betsey King Brunk, MMT, MT-BC

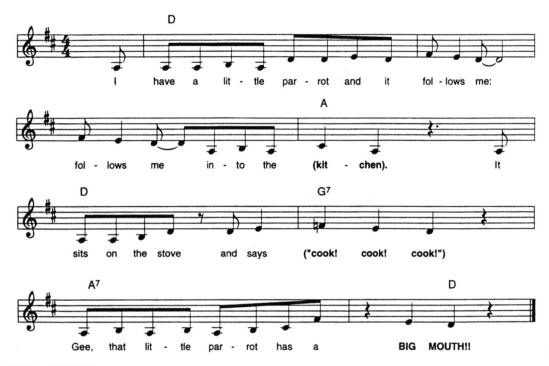

SUGGESTIONS: Use a parrot cut-out as a visual aid, as well as pictures of each room

Additional Verses:

I have a little parrot and it follows me: follows me: follows me into the bathroom.
It sits on the tub and says "wash, wash, wash!" (or "take a bath")
Gee, that little parrot has a BIGMOUTH!

I have a little parrot and it follows me: follows me: follows me into the living room.
It sits on the coach and says "sit, sit, sit!" (or "watch T.V.")
Gee, that little parrot has a BIG MOUTH!

I have a little parrot and it follows me: follows me: follows me into the classroom.
It sits on the desk and says "work, work, work!" (or "go to sleep")
Gee, that little parrot has a BIG MOUTH!

I have a little parrot and it follows me: follows me: follows me into the bedroom.
It sists on the bed and says "sleep, sleep, sleep!" (or "go to sleep")
Gee, that little parrot has a BIG MOUTH!

Copyright 1995
Kathleen Coleman, MMT, MT-BC and Betsey King, MMT, MT-BC
Prelude Music Therapy Products

Ravioli

Ra - vi - o - li, I love ra - vi - o - li,

Ra - vi - o - li, that's the stuff for me!

Did you get it on your (clothing)?

Yes, I got it on my (clothing).

On my (clothing)! On my (clothing)!

On my (clothing)! On my (clothing)! Oh! No!

These pictures symbols can be used with the "Ravioli" song. You can color and laminate them, and attach them to a file folder with Velcro™. You can create two sets of pictures and have students match them, You also can place these pictures on multi-cell augmentative communication devices like a rocking plate switch, so that students can make choices.

Skirt	**Shorts**	**Hat**
Underwear	**Pants**	**Shoes**
Shirt	**Socks**	**Pajamas**

Music Provides a Safe Place to Practice Social Skills

One of the primary issues for children in the autism spectrum is socialization. Music therapy strategies can provide a safe place to practice social skills.

One of the challenges of the social environment for a child on the autism spectrum is the inconsistency of each encounter. One visitor wants to shake hands, another does not. Some people say, "Hello, how are you?" but don't stick around for the answer. Socialization means interaction, and that means stepping out of one's comfort zone.

Songs and other musical experiences can assist a child with autism in practicing social skills and learning to initiate them as well. Songs are consistent. This provides security for students when they are working on socialization. Using music also helps the parent, teacher or therapist stay consistent in their interactions and presentations of information.

Music has always been a part of rituals and rites in various societies. In the society of autism, music can help a child remember some of the complicated "rules" of interaction.

A few years ago, I worked with a small "Total communication" class in a local school district. I provided a group music therapy session for the 5 boys who were in the class, two times per week. On the days that I was not there, the teacher sang many of the music therapy songs with the students.

Our sessions always started with a greeting song based on the melody "Pop Goes The Weasel."

Hello, I'd like to sing to you
I'd like to shake your hand.
My name is Betsey
Your name is_____

I sang this song with each member of the group, in turn. Then, going back to the first student, I sang "How Are You?"

"How Are You?" (printed at the end of this chapter) is based on the tune "Three Blind Mice." After asking the question at the start of the song, I had each student pick a picture symbol from a group of six indicating emotions. Each student would place his symbol into a sentence strip and use this to complete the song. I changed my accompaniment on the guitar to reflect the different feelings.

One of the first things that happened was that the students began to initiate their part in these opening socialization songs. Then, one day, we heard from one of the parents that their son had appropriately expressed his frustration for the first time by singing "I am mad! I am mad!" when he was not allowed to watch television when he wanted to.

Near the end of the school year an aide from another classroom in which I provided music therapy services approached me. She was also a bus driver for the district and transported some of the students in my Total Communication class. She told me about her experience with one of them, who I'll call Chris.

The previous afternoon, Chris came up the steps of the bus as usual. This time, however, he stopped in front of the driver and began to sing:

Hello, I'd like to sing to you
I'd like to shake your hand.
My name is Chris -
And your name is:

At this point, Chris extended his hand. The driver/aide shook his hand and said "Janelle." Chris immediately released her hand and began singing again.

How are you, Janelle?
How are you?

Chris had learned the "rules" of greeting someone from the opening songs of our sessions.

There are other ways in which music and songs can be used to support social interaction. Question and answer songs help students learn to listen and respond.

"What Did You Find?" (a song printed at the end of this chapter) is structured so that the leader asks a question with a melody that rises up. The responsive phrase, for the students to say, sign, or sing, moves downward and requires them to identify an object by color and name.

You also can create a song that asks a yes/no question and provides a place for the student to indicate his or her answer. (A Yes/No song in this format is available in the Prelude "Learning Through Music" Volume 3).

Another way in which music supports socialization is in instrument playing. This non-verbal communication can be a springboard to more traditional forms of interaction. I have a student that is non-verbal and does not consistently use an augmentative communication system. In the classroom and in his home, he does not always even show that he is listening to the speaker. However, when I roll his wheelchair up to the left end of a piano keyboard, he becomes an effective communicator. He plays a cluster of notes with one hand—I respond by playing another set of notes. When I imitate him correctly, he laughs. When I haven't played to his satisfaction, he takes my left wrist and makes me play the number of notes he wants. At the piano, he is an enthusiastic socializer.

Summary

- Music provides a safe, predictable place for children with autism to practice social skills.

- Using music for greetings and other interactions helps peers and adults keep their part of a social encounter consistent.

- Children can use songs to express their feelings, desires, and to initiate conversation.

- Some children can demonstrate more social skills in a non-verbal, instrumental setting than they can with more traditional methods.

How Are You?

Traditional
B. Brunk/S. Cartwright

What Did You Find?

What Did You Find?

Music Makes Repetition and Memorization Enjoyable

Anyone who has ever learned the alphabet by singing "The Alphabet Song" understands this use of music. Advertisers use music for this same reason: melody, harmony, and rhythm provide a concrete, memorable association for the information contained in a song. You probably have at least one phone number for a local business memorized as the result of one of their ads.

When it is important that a child learn a particular piece of information (a name, an address, a phone number), music may be an effective tool. While the ultimate goal is for the student to be able to produce the information without a musical cue, the use of music can accelerate the acquisition of the practice by using it on a daily basis. And, as discussed earlier, music makes repetition more palatable.

Considerations in Choosing and Adapting Songs

A song can be tenacious. Many of us have had the experience of hearing a tune over and over again in our minds, for no discernable reasons. A melody from our high school years trigger vivid memories. Music is such a strong stimulus that, on occasion, a child's first words come in a song. For several years, I worked with people recovering from traumatic brain injuries. In many cases, as they came out of coma, the first word they spoke were prompted by my singing a familiar song.

Most of the time, it doesn't matter that a song has lyrics that are mispronounced slightly, or that a phrase sounds different in a song than it does in speech. However, if a child with learning and communication difficulties learns important information through music, the information should be presented correctly.

"Piggyback" songs are those in which new lyrics are sung to a familiar melody. Teachers supply stores often sell books that include many piggyback songs: the days of the week set to "The Battle Hymn of the Republic," for example. Often, however, if you try to sing the words given to the song that has been suggested, you find yourself changing the emphasis of words, singing phrases in an awkward way, and holding out single syllables over several notes. Such songs may be harmless (and even helpful) for a regular education classroom, but if a child learns and retains information primarily through music, then mispronounced words and strange phrasing can be a problem.

Here is one commonly used piggyback song: a greeting set to the tune of "Good Night Ladies."

**He-llo Suzy
He-llo Suzy
He-llo Suzy
I'm glad you're here today.**

The problem is "hello." In regular speech, the emphasis is on the second syllable. If you sing it in this tune, however, the emphasis is on the first syllable. If student learns how to say hello with this song, a transition from using music to speech will be more difficult.

Here's another: the days of the week sung to "You Are My Sunshine."

**Sunday, Monday, Tuesday
Wednesday, Thursday, Friday,
And at the end comes Saturday...**

Notice how differently each day of the week is pronounced, while in speech, the emphasis in each word is quite similar.

Other interesting, and often amusing, things happen to words and phrases when they are imposed on a particular melody. I have heard songs in which a phrase such as "I'm walking up the stairs" is sung to a melody line that gets progressively lower and lower.

Another concern in selecting and adapting songs is the issue of where the most important information appears in the song. Problems in this area are not limited to piggyback songs: I often hear songs from professional children's recordings that pass over the key lyrics quickly and do not place them in a way that makes it easy for a child to hear and sing them.

The best placement for a key word in a song is at the end of a phrase. Remember the discussion of harmony and its use as a cue for responses? If an important word is placed on the final note/chord of a song, then the notes and chords that lead up to it can stop just before the last word and the student may be compelled to provide that word, just to hear the resolution of the music.

The fact that a word or phrase comes at the end of a lyric line also makes it possible for you to allow a long response time on the part of the student without making the song unrecognizable. In contrast, if the words that a student is supposed to be singing appear in the middle of a line, the song may be broken up so much that the benefit of using a song is lost. If the words appear at the beginning of a line, the song may never get off the ground!

Here is one more consideration: if a song is going to be a regular part of a student's life, it is important that, if possible, it be appropriate to his or her chronological age. Familiarity with popular musical styles can facilitate inclusion with peers. On the other hand, a junior high student who sings only pre-school songs will stand out as "different." It is possible to present information simply and repetitively without placing it in a "childish" context.

"Number Rock," which appears at the end of this chapter, is an example of a song that meets several criteria for therapeutic/educational songs. The lyrics repeat key information without unnecessary words, the most important words (the numbers) fall at the end of phrases and on strong beats, and the style of the song is appropriate for students of all ages.

A Checklist for Therapeutic Songs

Use these ten questions to evaluate the music you are using for therapeutic and/or educational purposes. Remember, some music is just for fun: These questions apply to those songs that you are going to use to assist a child in achieving non-musical, communication, academic, and social goals.

These questions will serve as a summary for this chapter.

1.   Do you really need a song?

Is this the best way to convey the information or motivate the student? Has the student shown you that he/she will respond particularly well to the structure and/or stimulation of music?

2.   Is the song age-appropriate?

No matter what the student's "cognitive age," it is disrespectful to continue to use nursery school music with, for example, a junior high school-age student. There are many songs out there that have a contemporary feel while maintaining simplicity in presentation of concepts.

3.   Are the range and key of the song appropriate?

Make sure that you know the range of your student's speaking voice—and use that as your guide in choosing the vocal range for songs. When using music therapeutically, it is far less important that songs be sung in "pretty" voices; it is far more important that the song is able respond naturally and automatically. In addition, if you remember to sing in the range of your speaking voice, you will be taking good care of your "instrument" and will be less fatigued at the end of a long day.

4. What would be the purpose of the song?

If you are going to use music for a therapeutic purpose, you need to choose songs for specific goals—that's the only way you'll be able to evaluate their effectiveness.

Mnemonics

Songs can be a great structure for things we need to remember, especially for information that is appropriate to be reproduced in a sing-song way (like a phone number).

Repetition

Music can make repetition more tolerable—doing a repeated physical exercise, or practicing the production of a consonant sound often will be less tedious for a student and therapist when accompanied by music.

Structure/motivation

Songs and music tasks can be structured so that they can only be completed if the student performs a particular skill—from moving a single finger to activate a sensitive switch, to reading lyrics from a book or chart. The strong motivation we all have to hear the completion of a melodic or harmonic phrase is an effective tool.

Attention-getting/maintaining

Music, and the contrasting silence, provides a powerful nonverbal cue for getting, and maintaining a student's attention. This can be a welcome break from oft repeated verbal or physical cues.

5. Is the text setting correct?

Are the words of the song pronounced as they would be in speech, both melodically and rhythmically? For many students, music is such a strong medium that you may find it difficult to help them "unlearn" poor prosody or articulation.

6. Are the key words and concepts placed correctly?

Check to see if the most important words are placed at the end of phrases and, if possible, cued by the harmony of the song.

7. Do you need an accompaniment for the song to be effective?

This is not a yes/no question—it is a reminder to be aware that the effectiveness of some songs is diminished when they are sung "a capella"—without accompaniment. If you use several songs in a session, they may begin to sound similar (and increasingly boring) if they are all sung without harmonic or rhythmic background. Harmony also helps students recognize songs.

8. What is the level of complexity in the song's lyrics, melody, accompaniment?

In most cases, simpler is better. Children, in particular, love to master song, and they do not mind if it is short and sweet. Besides, extra verbiage (like long verses and bridges) distracts from the key concepts you are trying to present or the key information the student needs to practice.

9. If you are using more than one song, do the styles have variety (tempo, keys, style, culture?

One of the reasons you choose to use music is its power to grab attention. If you vary the styles of your songs, your students will have something new to listen for at different points in the session and different topics will be distinct from one another.

10. Do you have a method for evaluating the effectiveness of the songs you are using?

If you are going to use music in therapy (even if it is just mean to be a diversion or distraction), you should consistently evaluate its effectiveness. If music is not providing your students with significant motivation or assistance in performing targeted skills, the you should investigate other educational methods and related services.

Number Rock

B. Brunk, MMT, MT-BC

Take Me Riding

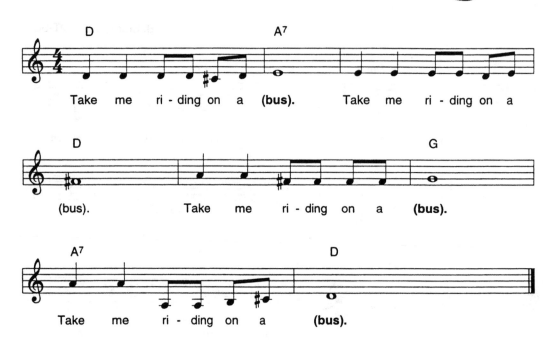

Music Lets Children Control Their Environment

There are three primary ways in which children can control their environments using music. First, children can choose recordings or musical videos to play. Second, as I described earlier, children can use a song to express a feeling or initiate a conversation.

Third, the use of simple rhythm instruments gives children a chance to alter their environment moment to moment. When I introduce a child to an instrument and he begins to experiment with it, I accompany him on guitar and play in the same way he is playing if aggressively, I play louder and faster. If he stops, I stop. After a session or two, many students begin to manipulate me; changing the way they play rapidly, to see if I can keep up! It is a pleasure to see a student take control when he is normally at the mercy of his environment.

Instruments

Instruments are a big part of music therapy. Why?

- Instruments allow a child to see where the sound is coming from.

- Instruments provide tactile stimulation that can be reinforcing or, in the same case of a child who is tactile sensitive, instruments can be a way to motivate that child to experience new sensations.

- Instruments provide an avenue for nonverbal communication.

- Instruments can be a non-threatening and easy way of participating in a social group—like a bell choir.

Many people ask me how children with autism respond to the sound of different instruments and music. A common question is, "What instruments should I avoid?"

The answer is that such preferences are completely individual. While I have found, over the years, that instruments that produce white noise (like a tambourine) are more likely to be irritating to a child in the autism spectrum, I have students with autism who love such instruments.

Many times, a student simply needs time to get used to a new sound. I have done music therapy assessments in which the student started out by covering her ears for any sound, and ended the session playing a drum loudly with a rock and roll guitar accompaniment.

What you need to know about rhythm instruments.

Many companies see boxes of rhythm instruments at "bargain prices." Although there are always exceptions, most of these kits contain instruments that are, at best, inadequate and at worst, dangerous.

For example, many of these instrument collections contain instruments that have tambourine jingles attached with a nail. Others can be disassembled easily, especially buy a child with autism. The parts are small enough to be swallowed and present a danger of choking. Instrument manufacturers do not come under the same scrutiny as toy makers. You must monitor the safety of the instruments that your children use.

Other instruments in such kits are simply inadequate. Drums are small and have no resonance, triangles and other bells are tinny sounding.

Although it may seem like a cost-effective measure to purchase large quantities of rhythm instruments at a discount, I believe you will be happier if you buy 3 or 4 performance-quality instruments. The next two pages will introduce you to some that you might consider for your classroom or home. Information on purchasing such instruments is available at the end of this book.

PLAY ALONG

Check the instruments that you may already have in your classroom or home. Be sure that they are safe for your children to use.

Cabasa

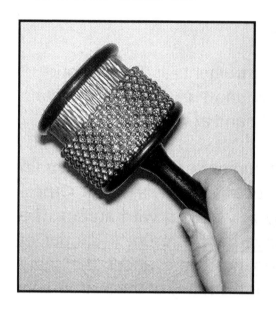

Metal beads around a wooden cylinder

Textural, visual

Different sizes

Transparent Rainstick

Visual

Different sizes

Available in rainbow colors

Kokoriko

Can be called a clatterpillar

Wooden slats

Is played like a "slinky"

Repetitive visual pattern

Paddle Drum

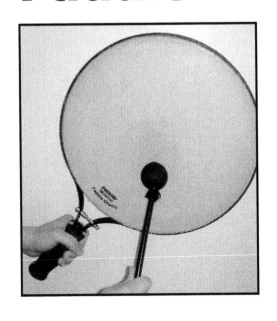

Resonant

Comes in lollipop styles

Can be pulled away quickly

Jingle Stick

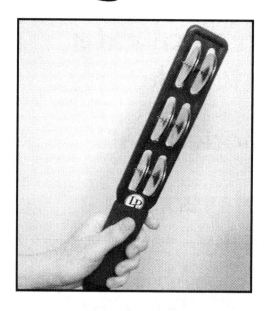

Pole with bells or tambourine disks

Durable

Entertaining

Textural, visual

Summary

- Children can control their environment using music.

- They can choose to play recorded music or videos with favorite songs.

- They can use songs to express feelings and/or initiate communication.

- Playing rhythm instruments is another way in which children can learn to control the environment.

- Teachers and parents must make sure that the instruments they use are safe.

- Visually interesting instruments are attractive to children with autism.

- Instrument preferences are individual and sometimes develop over time.

What Instrument?

B. Brunk, MMT-BC

What in - stru - ment will you choose to - day? What

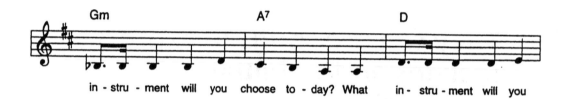

in - stru - ment will you choose to - day? What in - stru - ment will you

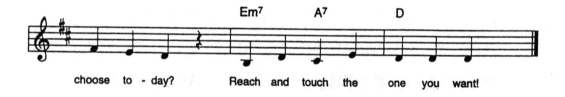

choose to - day? Reach and touch the one you want!

Music Can Create, or Emphasize, a Routine

Children on the autism spectrum usually benefit and respond positively to a set routine. However, when they participate in a class with children with different preferences—or when they are included in a class with peers in which there is less concern about a consistent routine from day to day, children with autism can become anxious and have difficulty concentrating.

Music can provide welcome cues for such children. Music therapist use music to identify different parts of the day, to make transitions between activities, and to accompany tasks with which their students have the most difficulty.

Included in this chapter are three "routine" songs. "I Have Five" highlights holidays and seasons; "The Hairbrushing Song" and "The Backpack Song" are for common activities.

Many teachers in pre-school and special-education classrooms have a time set aside for music. A child on the autism spectrum, however, might benefit more from having music parceled out throughout the day, signaling specific events ("time for lunch") or helping him make a change ("now we're done with reading; it's time to go to gym").

Parents are ingenious in this regard. At every conference I speak, I meat at least 3 or 4 parents who have made up songs to accompany toothbrushing! They have discovered that a song can make a less-preferred activity go more smoothly.

Children in the autism spectrum respond well to music at least partly because it stays the same from day to day. When a particular group of students arrives at music therapy, they know the music they will hear first: the greeting song.

Two years ago, I started working with a young man with autism for whom music is a primary learning modality. Most of his speech occurs during singing and the introduction of music into his environment is likely to help him calm down and focus.

One day last year, I entered the cafeteria of our school and found him in a highly agitated state. He was finished with his lunch, so I told his teacher I would take him for a walk. He led me Directly to the music therapy room. Once inside, he strummed my guitar, which was propped up on a chair, pulled a file folder activity from my bag, and sat in his usual seat.

I sat down and sang the greeting song. He was calm and participated as he always does. We did some additional music strategies and, about 10 minutes into our impromptu session, he began to get up and wander around. I responded by singing the "goodbye" song and he immediately returned to his seat so that the song would be completed in the usual manner. Music on this day, as it has on many others, provided this student with a safe, predictable place to be when he most needed it.

Summary

Music can provide consistent cues to emphasize the routine of a day.

Music can assist a student with transitions from one activity to another.

Music does not have to be presented at one specific time during the day. It can be used throughout the day to highlight a schedule, or accompany difficult tasks.

Play Your Instruments

B. Brunk, MMT, MT-BC

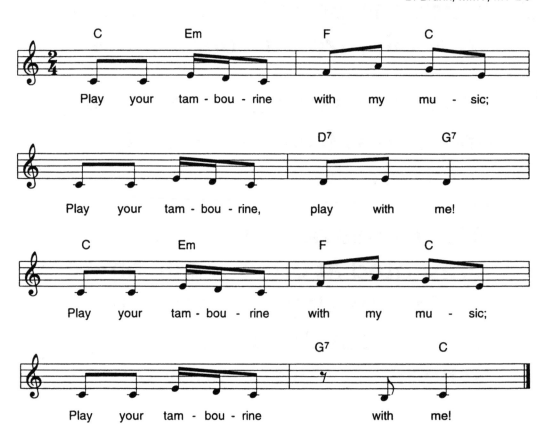

Play your tam - bou - rine with my mu - sic;

Play your tam - bou - rine, play with me!

Play your tam - bou - rine with my mu - sic;

Play your tam - bou - rine with me!

I Have Five

Betsey King Brunk, MMT, MT-BC

Hairbrush Song

Dedicated to Megan

K. Coleman, MMT, MT-BC

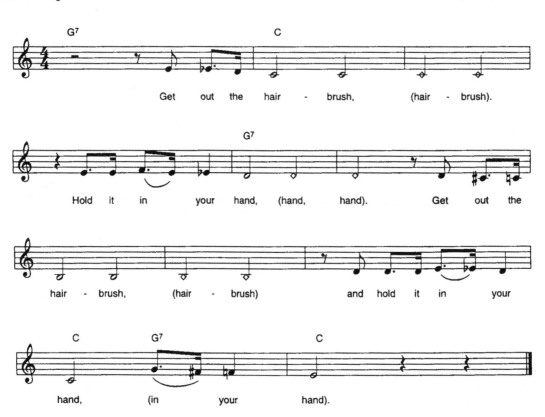

Get out the hair - brush, (hair - brush).

Hold it in your hand, (hand, hand). Get out the

hair - brush, (hair - brush) and hold it in your

hand, (in your hand).

Music Can Reflect and Adapt to Each Individual

One of the wonderful things about music—live music—is that as you play it with a group of children, you can change their reactions.

Earlier, I described how you might slow down or lower the volume on music when a student is over stimulted, or how you might leave longer pauses at certain points to allow students with a slow response time the opportunity to participate.

Other ways in which music can reflect and adapt to a child are (1) changing the lyrics of a song to spontaneously comment on a student's behavior, (2) singing back to a student those words or sounds he produces; and (3) accompanying a child's repetitive, self-stimulating behavior so as to make a connection and draw him out.

The kind of music therapy I have been describing with many my examples can be called "strategic" music therapy, in which songs are composed for specific purposes and students have paticular responses that they provide. Another form of music therapy intervention uses improvisation as its tool and is often known by the names of its founders, Nordoff-Robins (after Paul Nordoff and Clive Robins).

Improvisation is the production of music "on the spot." Improvised music may follow a certain chord progression, and it will usually have a steady beat, but it will sound different every time it is played. If you've ever heard a jazz concert, you've heard improvisation: the soloists take off from the original melody line and create their own interpretation.

In therapy, improvisation can be used to reflect clients' behavior, giving them instant feedback as to what they are doing, providing acceptance, and offering alternatives. For example, a music therapist may improvise music (on the piano or guitar) that accompanies a child's constant rocking. This rocking may be blocking any attempts at communication with the child. The improvisational music therapist might accompany that rocking, "entraining" as it were, with the child, communicating acceptance through the music. Very gradually (over many sessions, perhaps) the music therapist would make changes in the music and watch for them to be reflected in the child (changes in the speed of the rocking, or pauses that match or follow pauses in the music). This would lead to increasingly complex nonverbal communication (such as that which I described earlier with the young man and the piano), then verbal initiation, and so on.

Another example pf improvisational music therapy comes from a case of my own. Several years ago, I worked with a 36-year-old man with a dual diagnosis of autism and mental retardation who was living at home with his elderly mother. She had been reluctant, in the past, to placing him in a group home or state institutional setting, but was now going to have to do so. However, her sons behavior was uncooperative, and often violent, and she was having trouble finding a place that would accept him. On the advice of her caseworker, she brought in several therapists to work with him, to try and get him to cooperate with others and adapt to different routines.

This client (who I will call Robert) had loved playing music as a boy; in fact, he had at one point been able to play the melody for "The Star Spangled Banner" on the piano. At the time I started seeing him, however, the only auditory input he allowed besides his mother's voice was the television. He spent most of his day sitting at the kitchen table, picking at a meal and watching TV. Often, he was not fully clothed or properly dressed.

When I began coming to his house, Robert did not allow me to sit at the table with him and protested loudly (and unintelligible) if I tried to interrupt his routine. Therefore, for the first few weeks that I saw him, I sat in the living room, about 20 feet from him, eventually strumming my guitar quietly. Gradually, over a period of several sessions, he allowed me to move closer and closer until I was sitting at the table with him. I had begun singing improvisational songs about whatever he was doing. One day, after I had been seeing him for about two months, I was singing about him chewing his sandwich and he suddenly paused, mid-chew, and started to laugh. We had found our Contact Song (see chapter 1) and Robert had accepted my place in his environment.

Within 3 weeks, Robert was coming into the living room for his session, following a picture schedule for several activities, and had begun to attempt to play "The Star Spangled Banner" again.

Summary

- There are several ways you can use live music to reflect and adapt to a person's behavior and responses.

- You can spontaneously change lyrics to comment on a child's behavior.

- You can change the tempo of the music to either stimulate or calm a student.

- You can provide pauses that allow a student with a slow response time the opportunity to participate.

- Improvisational music therapy can be used to communicate acceptance of a person's behavior and to gradually invite them to interact with you.

Music Is Moveable

Once a child has learned a song and associated it with an activity, mood, behavior, or skill, that song can accompany the child into a variety of environments and provide a familiar, comforting and compelling cue. In this way music therapy can meet one of the goals of any therapy: to generalize the skills that are taught into a wider environment.

Music and the skills they accompany can be taken from school to home and from home to unfamiliar settings. Music is a way of "taking the rules with you" and gently but effectively reminding a child about new and old skills that they can use no matter where they are.

I work with several students each year on ambulation skills (in conjunction, of course, with their physical therapists, orientation and mobility specialists, etc.). For a girl with severe visual impairments that I've served for two years, I've composed songs that cue her for the proper use of her cane and for using buttons and snaps. For a boy who has trouble with grabbing at people and things as he walks down the hall, I've written a song reminding him of the balance techniques he's learned. In both cases, the parents of these students have learned the songs and use them at home and in community settings, like the mall and church.

Another example of mobile music is a song like "Making a Sandwich" (the music and visual aid pattern for this song are at the end of this chapter). Originally composed to work on sequencing and reading skills, this song has turned out to be a wonderful tool for some students to learn an important daily living skill. The only adjustment I needed to make was at the request of a mother who reported that her son would not attempt to make a sandwich at home unless she had every ingredient for which I had paper cutouts!

"The Stealing Song" (also printed at the end of this chapter) was originally composed for early childhood classes, but has also been effective as a song for my students with autism.

When making a song mobile, you may at first teach it by rote. The students will learn the lyrics and follow instruction simply through imitation and repetition. If you want the song to be effective as a generalization tool, you will have to take it into a functional environment. Instead of using visual aid cutouts, you will sing the "Sandwich Song" in a kitchen, for example.

Summary

- Music can be used to help a child take a skill from therapy or classroom to an unfamiliar environment.

- When parents and other people involved in a child's life learn these "mobile songs," they can provide the child with familiar cues, giving them the "rules" for a variety of situations.

- Mobile music can be used to remind a child about their own behaviors (the use of a cane, controlling the impulse to grab others) and to remind them about the behavior of others ("When I go to the mall, this is what happens.").

- To make a song mobile, you must eventually present it in the environment for which it is applicable.

Backpack Song

K. Coleman, MMT, MT-BC

Making a Sandwich

Betsey King Brunk, RMT-BC

These images can be used with the song "Making a Sandwich." They can be enlarged to fit in a file folder activity, or even more to go on a poster. Other than the cover art, the items should be individually cut out, colored and laminated so that the order of sandwich ingredients can change every time you sing the song.

The Stealing Song

B. Brunk, MMT, MT-BC

Part III: Music Therapy Services

How to find a qualified therapist; the facts about music therapy as a related service; and knowing what to ask for.

Here are some of the reasons you might consider using the services of a trained music therapist.

1. A music therapist is a musician first—and therefore has the skills to be flexible with music: changing tempos or keys, as we've discussed, or to be able to manipulate visual aids, maintain order, and play an instrument at the same time (in the same way that many teachers I know can manage 4 different augmentative devices, keep data, and communicate a lesson plan). You may find that your child or students have improved responses when a music therapist is able to adapt music specifically for them.

2. It is a music therapist's job to locate and know how to use a wide variety of musical styles, instruments and adaptations for those instruments. It is a music therapist's job to compose, adapt or locate specific songs or musical activities for specific goals for specific children. Parents and teachers have their hands full: sometimes it is a good use of time and money to have someone brought in who has easy access to the necessary resources.

3. A music therapist has been trained to plan, evaluate and document music therapy. For example, while teachers are especially tuned in to the behavior and skills they regularly document, I tend to notice things like the fact that Josh always heaves a heavy sigh and smiles as we move from the bridge to the final chorus of "What a Wonderful World." I can use that awareness of musical structure to motivate an increase in his attention for the math work we're doing) I also notice that Kelleen's head is nodding each 4th beat, indicating that she is

attending, even though there is no eye contact or vocalization; and that Paul sings 80% of the lyrics to songs in the key of G, and only 10% for songs in the key of D.

What to expect from a music therapist

- A music therapist will have current credentials, indicated by the letters MT-BC (see Part 1: A Qualified Music Therapist").

- A music therapist will adhere to good standards of practice, as outlined by the American Music Therapy Association (AMTA) and to that association's code of ethics. Copies of these documents are available from AMTA.

- Among the standards of practice that a music therapist should demonstrate are the following:

    1. Individualized assessments for each client

    2. Recommendations for or against therapy based on the assessment

    3. Written, time-specific goals and objectives for each client

    4. A written treatment plan that specifies music therapy strategies and techniques that will be used to address the goals and objectives

    5. Regular music therapy sessions with strategies and techniques that adhere to the treatment plan

6. Regular re-evaluation of the effectiveness of the interventions being used

7. Written documentation of progress and evaluation

8. Dismissal of the client from music therapy when services are no longer necessary or appropriate.

- The music therapist will be able to discuss a therapy plan with professionals and family members, relating it both to current music therapy practice and the client's specific needs.

- The music therapist will keep regular hours, give prompt notification of changes in the schedule or absences, and arrange to make up missed sessions if appropriate.

- The music therapist will work only within his or her area of expertise (music therapy) and will co-treat with another professional when treatment involves therapeutic issues other than the professional's domain.

- Music therapists will maintain appropriate therapeutic boundaries with their clients and honor the administrative structure of the school, institution or facility at which they work. The music therapist will maintain strict confidentiality.

- The music therapist will give adequate notice when relocating when circumstances require that services be transferred to another therapist. The music therapist will make every effort to assist in locating other MT-BC's, and will participate in the hiring process when appropriate.

- The music therapist will bill only for services that he or she has directly provided or supervised by agreement with the client or facility.

- The music therapist will demonstrate energy and enthusiasm for clients/students through:

    1. A caring and professional attitude

    2. The creative production of appropriate materials and strategies

    3. Networking with other music therapists

    4. Seeking out professional learning opportunities.

Adapted Music Lessons

How are adapted music lessons different from music therapy?

Music therapy is the use of music and music-related strategies to work on non-musical goals. Music therapy is practiced by board-certified specialists who have learned how to use music for cognitive, physical, and emotional goals. Music therapy usually will not focus on a single instrument—it will involve a variety of music strategies. Music therapists must set specific goals and objectives for designated time periods, and must document progress in writing.

Adapted music lessons, like all music education programs, focus on teaching musical skills, such as proficiency on an instrument, or appreciation and understanding of musical styles. Adapted music lessons may be provided by music educators (like piano teachers) or music therapists who have a background in pedology. The assessment, documentation, and evaluation procedures may be less extensive for music lessons.

How are adapted music lessons and music therapy alike?

Both adapted music lessons and music therapy may have an influence on a child's self-esteem, social skills, and other non-musical areas. Both approaches are based on the love of, and natural attraction to music that many children have.

How do I know if my child will be able to participate in adapted music lessons?

The answer to this question can come from two different sources; your knowledge of your child's strengths and weaknesses, and a trial period of instruction with a music teacher. Learning to play an instrument requires, among other things:

1. The ability to follow simple instructions

2. Some degree of fine motor control and coordination

3. The ability to store and recall information from one lesson to another.

A music teacher who offers adapted music lessons will look at these skills and may offer a trial period during which everyone involved can see how your child would respond. Much will depend on the instrument that is chosen—each one requires different abilities.

Children who have a disability that does not involve cognitive deficits may be best served by a music educator so that they may interact with age-level peers as part of the music studio or class. Children with cognitive deficits and/or multiple disabilities who desire adapted music lessons may be best served by a music therapist trained in creating successful experiences for clients with special needs.

How do I find a teacher who can give adapted music lessons?

Try contacting a music educator at your child's school for the names of teachers. Another source is a local music teacher's association. Music therapist in your area also may have the names of some qualified professionals. Ask your friends and neighbors for the names of teachers they know—then start the interview process.

The most important thing to remember is that, despite someone's qualifications to teach music in a traditional setting, he or she may not have experience in working with a child with special needs. You, as a parent, may not be a musician—but you are an expert on your child, and you should listen to your instincts as you interview and/or observe potential teachers.

Ask yourself: Can this teacher break down skills into smaller tasks that my child can master? Does this teacher have patience with unpredictable behavior? Does this teacher use positive reinforcement, and will he or she use it with greater frequency if my child needs it? Is this teacher comfortable with a slower rate of progress than that which other students may achieve? (Many children in adapted music lessons make the same progress as students in "regular sessions" but do it over a longer period of time.)

My child LOVES music, but adapted music lessons have not worked out. What can I do?

Music therapy may be an alternative for your child. As well as being a related service in many school systems, and a part of some agency programs, music therapy is offered as private therapy. When you contract privately for music therapy, you should participate in setting the goals and objectives for the sessions—and if the most important thing is that your child "have fun with music," the music therapist should enthusiastically plan with that in mind. Music therapists use instruments, songs, music software, and a variety of music-based strategies to work on your child's non- musical goals—but you can request that a particular instrument be a part of the sessions, so that your child has an opportunity to hear it and participate in playing it. One of the benefits of music therapy as a therapeutic tool for children is that, whatever the goal (cognitive, communication, physical), it is almost always fun!

Five Things to Know and Remember about Music Therapy in the Public Schools:

1. "Music therapy is a related service." This was originally stated in the congressional report on IDEA and it has been affirmed by the Federal Office of Special Education.

2. The only way for music therapy to be placed on an IEP as a related service is through an assessment conducted by a qualified music therapist.

3. Music therapy may be provided as an educational consult service to a group of students (early childhood or autism programs, for example), and this may provide more children with service and teachers with materials they can use on a daily basis, but it should not be listed as a related service on any student's IEP if that student has not received an individualized assessment.

4. An assessment for music therapy as a related service should, at minimum, include a review of the student's current IEP, interviews with key IEP team members, and an assessment process/instrument that provides specific data as to whether or not music therapy makes a significant difference in a student's ability to benefit from his or her IEP.

5. The standard for recommending music therapy in the public schools (according to the federal law) is usually more stringent than that for therapy in other settings. While a child may enjoy music and even "benefit" from the inclusion of music in education and therapy, in order for music therapy to be recommended as a related service, it must be "required" for a child to benefit from his or her special education program.

To locate music therapist near you:

Contact
The American Music Therapy
Association (AMTA)
at
(301) 589-3300
http://www.musictherapy.org

References

Adamek, M. & Darrow, A.A. (2003). *Music in Special Education.* Silver Spring, MD: American Music Therapy Association.

Berger, D.S. (2001). *Music Therapy, Sensory Integration, and the Autistic Child.* Philadelphia: Jessica Kingsley.

Buday, E. (1995). "The effects of signed and spoken words taught with music on sign and speech imitation by children with autism." *Journal of Music Therapy, 32,* 189-202.

Brownell, M.D. (2002). "Musical adapted social stories to modify behaviors in students with autism: four case studies." *Journal of Music Therapy, 39,* 117-144.

Bruscia, K. (1999). *Case Studies in Music Therapy.* Gilsum, NH: Barcelona.

Edgerton, C.L. (1994). "The effect of improvisational music therapy on the communicative behaviors of autistic children." *Journal of Music Therapy, 31,* 31-62.

Furman, C. (2001). *Effectiveness of Music Therapy Procedures: Documentation of research and clinical practice.*

Griggs-Dane, E.R., and Wheeler, J.J. (1997). "The use of functional assessment procedures and individualized schedules in the treatment of autism: Recommendations for the music therapist." *Music Therapy Perspectives, 15,* 87-93.

Nelson, D. L. (1984). "Music activities as therapy for children with autism and other pervasive developmental disorders." *Journal of Music Therapy*, 21, 100-116.

Thaut, M.E., (1988). "Measuring musical responsiveness in autistic children: A comparative analysis of improvised musical tone sequences of autistic, normal, and mentally retarded individuals." *Journal of Autism and Developmental Disorders*, 18, 561-571.

Whipple, J. (2004). "Music in intervention for children and adolescents with autism: A meta-analysis." *Journal of Music Therapy*, 40, 90-106.

Wilson, B. (2001). *Models of Music Therapy Interventions in School Settings: From institution to inclusion.* Silver Spring, MD: American Music Therapy Association.

Prelude Music Therapy

The songs and visual aids featured in this book are taken from the materials offered by Prelude Music Therapy, co-owned by Betsey King, MMT, MT-BC, and Kathleen Coleman, MMT, MT-BC.

For information on the songbooks, therapy materials, and workshops produced by Prelude, which are appropriate for pre-school & special education teachers, music therapists, and music educators, please visit:

www.preludemusictherapy.com

The Prelude Music Therapy website also has information on music therapy in the public schools, music therapy research, and tips for music in therapy and education.

CPSIA information can be obtained
at www.ICGtesting.com
Printed in the USA
LVHW061516211019
634863LV00001B/33/P